T0196487

Poems

to Comfort, Encourage and Inspire

ANGEL OPHELIA

WESTBOW
PRESS®
A DIVISION OF THOMAS NELSON
& ZONDERVAN

WestBow Press books may be ordered through
booksellers or by contacting:

WestBow Press
A Division of Thomas Nelson & Zondervan
1663 Liberty Drive
Bloomington, IN 47403
www.westbowpress.com
1 (866) 928-1240

Because of the dynamic nature of the Internet, any web addresses or
links contained in this book may have changed since publication and
may no longer be valid. The views expressed in this work are solely those
of the author and do not necessarily reflect the views of the publisher,
and the publisher hereby disclaims any responsibility for them.

Any people depicted in stock imagery provided by Thinkstock are models,
and such images are being used for illustrative purposes only.
Certain stock imagery © Thinkstock.

Scripture quotations taken from the King James Version.

ISBN: 978-1-5127-6610-3 (sc)
ISBN: 978-1-5127-6609-7 (e)

Library of Congress Control Number: 2016919624

Print information available on the last page.

WestBow Press rev. date: 09/09/2019

Preface

The inspirational writings that you will read in this book came from a deep knowledge within my spirit; thoughts coming from a place within me that I had never visited before bringing me great peace and joy.

I was in tune with the Holy Spirit and delighted greatly in giving praise, honor, and glory to God.

I am hoping that these inspirational words will bless you as they have blessed me.

To God be the glory always.

Poems

to Comfort, Encourage and Inspire

Only Believe

My God has never ever failed
To let His glory show.
To eyes and hearts that seek and search
He'll open every door.

Don't ever fail to venture out
Beyond your fondest dream,
Although dark clouds may fill the air,
Your soul has been redeemed.

Jesus Christ has paid the price
The victory has been won.
So claim your prize, and lift your eyes
Give thanks to God's dear Son.

For God so loved the world that he gave
His only begotten son that who so ever
Believeth in him shall not perish but have
Everlasting life.

—John 3:16

Have Faith

When God gives us a blessing
It's unique in every way,
And sometimes we may wonder
If this good is here to stay.

And just briefly, for a moment
We ponder o'er what we see,
And then we think, this is from God.
I know it is complete.

My heart rejoice in gladness
For what I've seen and heard.
My God I know will always be
True and faithful to His word.

Trust in the Lord with all your heart
Lean not to your own understanding.

—Proverbs 3:5

Trust in His Name

Jesus is the only name
To take you through the plight.
No matter where you go or search
No other will be right.

It was Jesus stretched upon the cross
And gave His life for you,
And Jesus is the only one
Who can go to God for you.

There is no other name
Except the name of Jesus Christ,
So don't be fooled by others
Who tell you theirs are right.

For your salvation is at stake
Just know in whom you trust,
For God's dear Son is the only One
Who died for all of us.

For God so loved the world that He gave his only
begotten Son that whosoever believeth in Him
shall not perish but have everlasting life.
—John 3:16

Time

If I rush to start the day,
Who'll be there to point the way?

Will my efforts be in vain
If I don't have His helping hand?

I must prepare before I start
If I want Him to do His part.
Pay attention to what I say:
Pray before you start your day.

*Trust in the lord with all thine heart and lean not
To thine own understanding, in all thy ways
acknowledge him and he shall direct your paths.*

—Proverbs 3:5–6

My Child

I say to you, you are my child.
So why do you wonder where art thou ?
I'm never far away from you.
I'll always help you think things through.

I've never failed you in the past.
My love for you will always last.
No matter what it seems to be,
My Spirit will always set you free.

You are my child, I love you so,
That's why I'll never let you go.

I'll never leave nor forsake you.

—Hebrews 13:5

Be Grateful

Just when you think that things are right
And you are on your way,

The sun is bright
A great delight
Makes for a special day.

You look way deep
Into the sky
And see a cloud or two,

You start to wonder in your mind
The things that brought you through

The Grace of God,
Oh, what a gift that He has given all.

Humble yourself in gentleness,
Pride comes before the fall.

My grace is sufficient for you.
—2 Corinthians 12:19

Jesus Saves

I thank you, God, for Jesus Christ,
Your only begotten Son.

He came to earth to die for us
So victories can be won.

He stretched His arms
And bowed His head
And said that it is finished.

The curtains were rent,
And heaven was meant
To all of God's own children.

There is no greater love I know
As great as my dear Father,

Who made a way through Jesus Christ
To save His sons and daughters.

*For God so loved the world that He gave his only
begotten Son that whosoever believeth in Him
shall not perish but have everlasting life.*

—John 3:16

Search

When life is running to and fro
And you don't know which way to go,
Attune yourself to God within
Who washes away unrighteous sin.

You must be still and let it go,
You have a friend within, you know.
Cast all imaginations down,
And wipe away that awful frown.

You'll have the victory in the end,
So be aware He bore all your sins.
You point your finger at your brother,
It's easy just to blame another.
But turn your eyes within yourself,
And go and seek your Father's help.

*Greater is He that's within me then he that is
in the world.*

—1 John 4:4

Trust

I call upon His name up high,
And suddenly He's at my side.

A fresh-felt breeze engulfs my soul
And comforts me beyond control.

That's when I know my heart's at rest,
For then I feel His gentleness.

All tears have ceased and worries gone.
I know my God is on His throne.

So I will rest within His love,
For I've been born from up above.

What shall we then say to these things?
If God be for us, who can be against us?
—Romans 8:31

Hold On

Oh how heavy a heart can be,
But I'm here to tell you He'll set you free.
No matter the trouble, no matter the pain,
I'm here to tell you He's healing again.

The time of old is His time of new.
What He's done in the past
In the future He'll do too.
Hold on to His hand no matter the pain.
My Jesus will help you time and time again.

For He shall give His angels charge over
you, to keep you in all your ways.

—Psalm 91:11

Family Blessing

God, bless our family.
Sometimes we're far apart.
Although we're great in distance,
We're centered in God's heart.

God, bless our family members
To love you and obey
Each and every hour
And minute of the day.

We know Your love is with us
To lift us when we fall,
Thank God our precious Jesus
Endured us on the cross.

If God be for you who can be against you.

—Romans 8:31

THE POTTER

A jewel hangs in the balance,
A rare stone to be cut.
Though edges may be jagged,
It's a diamond in the rough.

The tools of life will shape it,
Making such a precious stone
So deep, so sweet, so incomplete.
It rests in God's dear arms.

But when the stone is polished
And its brightness hits the light
Oh! What a sight to behold
You'll see God's brilliant light.

And we know that all things work
Together for good to them that love God,
to them who are the called according to His purpose.
—Romans 9:28

Be Still

Sometimes when things feel out of reach
And prayers you begin to repeat,

Not realizing patience has her way
To bring you to a brighter day.

You toss and turn and go your way
And hope the answer came yesterday.

The fight gets tough and it seems so long,
And then you feel God's loving arms.

You shout and say, "I thank You, Lord.
Thank You for hearing me when I call."

Be still and know that I am God.

—Psalm 46:10

VICTORY

Get off my back, I said out loud,
And ward away the dreary clouds
Arising on my heart afloat,
Making it hard for me to cope,

For darkness has no place in me.
I am a child of God, you see.
Wherever I am, darkness goes,
For I have peace within my soul.

I have no reason to feel lost.
My Jesus died upon the cross.
I have the victory in Him, you see,
My Jesus lives inside of me."

Greater is He that's in me then He that is in the world.
—1 John 4:4

Angel

How can you tell an angel?
Can you tell them by a smile?
Or can you tell them when you're burdened
And they'll help you to survive.

Oh yes! Sometimes it's serious,
And life is at your throat.
They'll enter with their presence
Allowing you to cope.

How can you tell an angel?
It's not so hard, you see.
Open your eyes, and you'll be surprised
The person you will see.

We entertain angels unaware.

—Hebrews 13:2

No Ending

How much do I love you?
I guess I'll never know.
Each time I try to count the time
I can never keep the score.

With all my heart I'm counting
To do my very best.
There is no ending to my love,
So I can never guess.

Because it's never-ending,
My love goes on and on,
And when I try to sum it up
That's when I'm proven wrong.

Then let me hold my treasure
Deeply buried in my heart,
And let it keep and guide me,
For that is where it starts.

For love is but reflections
That shine within our lives,
That light the way for others,
Depending on our guide.

Let us all be beacons
For everyone to see.
Our love will be discovered,
It will shine through you and me.

Love thy neighbor as thy self for the love of thee.
—Matthew 22:39

Free

You are so very wonderful
My mind just can't conceive.

The things you've done
And yet to come,
My heart rejoice and believe.

With eyes gazing up to heaven,
From there Your Son will come.

The trump will sound and gather us around,
God's children have overcome.

A joyous day will then begin.
Rejoice, I say, rejoice.

The King is here, so have no fear.
The victory has been won!

He who the Son set free is free in deed.

—John 8:36

Give Him the Victory

Oh God, you seem to come around
When things seems so unfair.
Your love, your peace, your mercy
Seems to filter out the air.

Of pressures fallen on our shoulders
We know not whence they come.
We thank You for the job we know
Inside's already done.

You soothe our souls and make us whole
By belief in Your dear Son.
We raise our heads and sing of praise.
The battle has been won.

He said He's conquered everything
From death, hell, and the grave,
For He is the great I Am,
And I'm His child who's saved.

If God be for you who can be against you.

—Romans 8:31

Give Thanks

I feel His Holy presence
Arresting on my soul.
Joy arises in my heart.
My cup overflows.

How deep is His perfection?
My mind can scarcely know.
You are my God Almighty.
You open every door.

Although the clouds seems heavy
And darkness fills the way,
The precious light from His delight
Will brighten up my day.

I bow down in submission
To honor His holy Word.
My feet are guided by His way.
My mind is not disturbed.

Now I am truly happy
In each and every way.
I thank my Father up above
For blessing me today.

To God be the glory.

—Romans 16:27

Let God

When your heart is heavy
And filled with despair,
I know a Savior who really, really cares.

He'll fix your wants and heal your needs,
He'll give you anything you please.

There is no limit to His love,
For He was sent from up above.

He loves us more than we can know,
That's why I'll never let Him go.

He who dwelleth in the secret place of the most
High, shall abide under the shadow of the almighty.
—Psalm 91:1

Prayer Answered

There's time when faith steps before you
And beckons time to come.

Despite your natural feelings,
You'll feel it's all been done.

And faith speaks right back at you
And says, "I know the way."

Decisions grip your very soul,
And you begin to pray.

You rise to the occasion,
And a light begins to shine,

And all those natural feelings
Are left in olden times.

You wave your flag in victory,
For now you see the way.

Just think what could have happened
Had you forgot to pray.

Praying always with all prayer and supplications in the Spirit.
                                                    —Ephesians 6:18

Coming Together

There seems to be a reaching out
To gather all the times
A wonderment with loving scent,
A joining of the minds,

A cleansing of the many hearts,
A lift from heaviness,
To soar way high above the clouds,
To find its place of rest.

Awake, O sleeper, deep within.
The time has finally come
To spread your wings and sing of things
Now here and yet to come.

*The Lord Himself will descend from heaven with a
shout, with the voice of an archangel, and with the trump
of God. And the dead in Christ will rise first. Then we
who are alive and remain shall be caught up together
with them in the clouds to meet the Lord in the air.*

—Thessalonians 14:16–17

Aim High

It's nice to go into your mind,
What love, joy, and peace you'll find.
Because you know you are complete.
Your sturdy soul knows no defeat.

A warrior that you are at heart.
You are a winner from the start.
You square your shoulders and lift your chin,
And, oh, what peace you'll feel within.

Don't stop and sigh in great defeat.
Those lesions surely you'll repeat.
Because you know Christ is the way,
Look forward to a brighter day.

I can do all things through Christ Jesus who strengthens me.
—Philippians 4:13

Blessed

When God gives us a blessing
It's unique in every way,
And sometimes we may wonder
If this good is here to stay.

Just briefly, for a moment
We ponder o'er what we see,
And then we say, "This is of God.
I know it is complete."

My heart rejoice in gladness
For what I've seen and heard.
My God I know will always be
True and faithful to His Word.

*For I am the Lord, your God, who takes hold of your right
hand and says to you, do not fear; I will help you.*
—Isaiah 41:13

Pray

There seems to be a time of day
When people go about their way.
The day is calm, the sun is down,
And people seem to scamper around.

Each going their separate ways,
I wonder if they stopped to pray,
To give the honor, praise, and thanks
To He who's highest in the ranks.

He reaches down from high above
And bless us with His precious love.
Jehovah You will always be
From now until eternity.

Jesus Christ the same yesterday, and today and forever.
—Hebrews 13:8

Laughter

A sister who is wise
And funny in every way,
Because she knows that laughter
Will brighten up your day.

Because she is a child of God
And wants to be a blessing,
She tells a joke because she knows
Laughter is God's own medicine.

She'll put you in a happy mood
And lift a heavy heart.
Then she'll go on smiling
because she's done her part.

A ministry within itself,
A gift to make one happy,
Such joy, love, and peace
Can be found in God's loving laughter.

A merry heart does good like a medicine,
but a broken spirit dries the bones.

—Proverbs 17:22

Family Prayer

God, bless our family.
Sometimes we're miles apart.
Although we're great in distance,
We are centered in God's heart.

God, bless our family members
To love You and obey
Each and every hour
And minute of the day.

We know Your love is with us
To lift us when we fall.
Thank God our precious Jesus
Endured us on the cross.

God is love.

—1 John 4:8

Graduation

While others went to party,
Your head was in the book,
And now you are rewarded
It's not by hook or crook.

Your endurance is a blessing.
It's God who shows the way,
And you were wise to follow Him
Each minute of the day.

I tip my hat in honor
For all that you have done.
Because you did the battle
The victory has been won.

O give thanks unto the Lord; for He is good:
for His mercy endureth forever.

—Psalms 136:1

My Son

A precious little angel God put into my hands.
A little bouncing baby boy has grown to be a man.

It seems like only yesterday I held him in my arms,
To comfort him in every way, and weather all his storms.

With Gods true words that I have heard I offered them
to him. And now God lives within his heart
He has the will to win.

I can do all things through Christ Jesus who strengthens me.
—Philippians 4:13

Happy Birthday Daughter

You're as precious as a flower
That blooms each day in spring.
Your smile is bright with sweet delight
That makes the birdies sing.

That's why I'll always celebrate
This good and joyous day
To say I love you very much
And have a HAPPY BIRTHDAY

O give thanks unto the Lord for He is good.
—1 Chronicles 16:34

My Friend

My friend you are to me indeed.
You always fill my every need.
No matter if the times seem rough,
In You I'll always put my trust.

The storms may rage,
And winds will blow,
I'll cry to you from here below.
And you will always hear my mourn,
Then suddenly all hurts are gone.

The Lord is good and his mercy
endured forever.

—Psalm136:1

Graduation Day

The time has come for you to say
I made it in a special way.

Though times were tough
And days were long,

You hung in there and weathered the storm.
So toss your cap, and have your way.

This is your graduation day!

May God bless you always.

My Husband

My husband is the kind of man
Who loves the Lord so dear.

My husband is a man who does not
live in constant fear.

My husband is the kind of man
Who comes to me from God,

The kind of man who would not make
Life's journey rough and hard.

My husband stands tall and strong,
For he lives by God's own Word.

He is not blown to and fro.
He knows in whom he serves.

He who findeth a wife findeth a good thing.
—Proverbs 18:22

Little Sister

Our sister who is loving
And kind in every way,
A heart of joy she brought to us
In each and every day.

When she was in our presence
Sunshine seemed to come.
The joy we shared can't be compared
To all we've ever done.

For she was always giving,
It brought her great delight.
To say, "This is for you,"
Then smile with all her might.

Where can we find another kind of love
So fair and true? It's in our little sister
God gave to me and you.

God is love.

—1 John 4:8

Save the Children

They came to my house not long ago,
Taking my children who wished not to go.
Against their will she took them away,
Saying she will bring them back maybe another day.

Little did she know that God's in the plan
To free the babies from her kind of hands.
No matter how clever her words may be,
Nothing goes on that my God can't see.

Despite of her lies and deceitfulness,
My God will put her to the test,
And what He does she'll truly see.
My God has always protected me.

No weapon formed against me shall prosper.
—Isaiah 54:17

My Sister

My sister is a special friend
Who's near and dear to heart.
Whenever there's a bill to fill,
She'll always play her part.

In many ways she's never failed
To give the right direction.
She'll filter through the rubbish
And bring it to perfection.

Because her mind is set all times
To shine the light to see,
That's why she is a joy to life
And she will always be.

*A man that has friends must show himself friendly and
there is a friend that sticketh closer than a brother.*
—Proverbs 18:24

God Is Good

Thank You, God, for this blessed day.
Thank You, God that you made a way
To walk us through this distant plight
And gave Your Son to make it right.

For all the joys You have foretold,
They now begin to unfold.
What a beacon I can see.
Your Spirit lives inside of me.

The Lord is good and his mercy endured forever.
—Psalm 100:5

A Warrior

The first that was born to me
It doesn't seem that long.
A precious, loving baby girl,
Who's now already grown.

She made her way through trials and snares
With strength that comes from God.
Despite the curves life tried to throw,
She called upon the Lord.

I'm proud to say
She is a soldier on God's own battlefield.
In faith she continues in His Word.
In Him does she believe.

A warrior she will always be
Up to the pearly gates.
I know in Him she will always pray
And keep the faith.

*Trust in the Lord with all your heart and
lean not to your own understanding.*

—Proverbs 3:5

Happy Birthday Sis

I didn't forget your birthday,
No matter what they say.
The moments, days, and hours,
They sometimes slip away.
But this I know God's with you,
In spite of my delay.

The things that are important,
They go and come each day,
But why I will remember
A special day is new

Because God has His hand on you
To always see you through.
So joy be with you always,
And peace be in your heart.

I've wished you happy birthday
Through love within a thought.

May God bless you always.

You Are Special

A fragrance that is sweet and true,
A heart that's sunshine warming too,
A fresh breeze that's gentle and kind,
So many things that make you shine.
The things you do in a special way
Makes me proud to say

HAPPY BIRTHDAY!!!

Because he has set his love upon me,
therefore will I deliver him.

—Psalms 91:14

Printed in the United States
By Bookmasters